Date: 7/3/18

J 947.7 VAS
Vasilyeva, Anastasiya,
Ukraine /

Ukraine

by Anastasiya Vasilyeva

Consultant: Karla Ruiz, MA
Teachers College, Columbia University
New York, New York

BEARPORT
PUBLISHING

New York, New York

Credits

Cover, © Evgeniy Fesenko/Dreamstime and © Ljupco/Shutterstock; TOC, © Ryzhkov Sergey/Shutterstock; 4, © mujdatuzel/iStock; 5T, © Tarasenko Nataliia/Shutterstock; 5B, © Simon Podgorsek/iStock; 7, © Tijuana2014/iStock; 8–9, © Moisieiev Igor/Shutterstock; 9B, © Arsgera/Shutterstock; 10, © smereka/Shutterstock; 11, © Sean Sprague/Alamy; 12, © VectorPlotnikoff/Shutterstock; 13, © Orest lyzhechka/Shutterstock; 14, © Eight Photo/Shutterstock; 15T, © Steve Morgan/Alamy; 15B, © Ihar Byshniou/iStock; 16–17, © vvoe/Shutterstock; 17TR, © Yulia Grigoryeva/Shutterstock; 18, © A_Lesik/Shutterstock; 19T, © Michael knowles/Alamy; 19B, © Repina Valeriya/Shutterstock; 20, © Oleh_Slobodeniuk/iStock; 21, © Alex Brylov/Shutterstock; 22, © Mikheyev Viktor/Shutterstock; 23, © Oksana Struk/iStock; 24–25, © vodograj/Shutterstock; 26, © katatonia82/Shutterstock; 27, © epa european pressphoto agency b.v./Alamy; 28T, © bhofack2/iStock; 28B, © Maya Morenko/Shutterstock; 29, © Joe Gough/Shutterstock; 30T, © Andrey Nekrasov/Alamy and © Aptyp_koK/Shutterstock; 30B, © Xinhua/Alamy; 31 (T to B), © joyfull/Shutterstock, © Orest lyzhechka/Shutterstock, © oneinchpunch/Shutterstock, © Travel Stock/Shutterstock, © Kristina Postnikova/Shutterstock, and © A_Lesik/Shutterstock; 32, © Eatmann/Shutterstock.

Publisher: Kenn Goin
Editor: Jessica Rudolph
Creative Director: Spencer Brinker
Design: Debrah Kaiser
Photo Researcher: Thomas Persano

Library of Congress Cataloging-in-Publication Data

Names: Vasilyeva, Anastasiya., author.
Title: Ukraine / by Anastasiya Vasilyeva.
Description: New York, New York : Bearport Publishing, 2017. | Series:
  Countries we come from | Includes bibliographical references and index. |
  Audience: Ages 5–8.
Identifiers: LCCN 2016042363 (print) | LCCN 2016043346 (ebook) | ISBN
  9781684020591 (library) | ISBN 9781684021116 (ebook)
Subjects: LCSH: Ukraine—Juvenile literature. | Ukraine—History—Juvenile
  literature. | Ukraine—Civilization—Juvenile literature.
Classification: LCC DK508.515 .V37 2017 (print) | LCC DK508.515 (ebook) | DDC
  947.7—dc23

LC record available at https://lccn.loc.gov/2016042363

For more information, write to Bearport Publishing Company, Inc., 45 West 21st Street, Suite 3B, New York, New York 10010. Printed in the United States of America.

10 9 8 7 6 5 4 3 2 1

Contents

This Is Ukraine 4

Fast Facts.................30

Glossary 31

Index 32

Read More 32

Learn More Online 32

About the Author 32

This Is Ukraine

MODERN

4

HUGE

Festive

5

Ukraine is a large country in Europe. More than 45 million people live there.

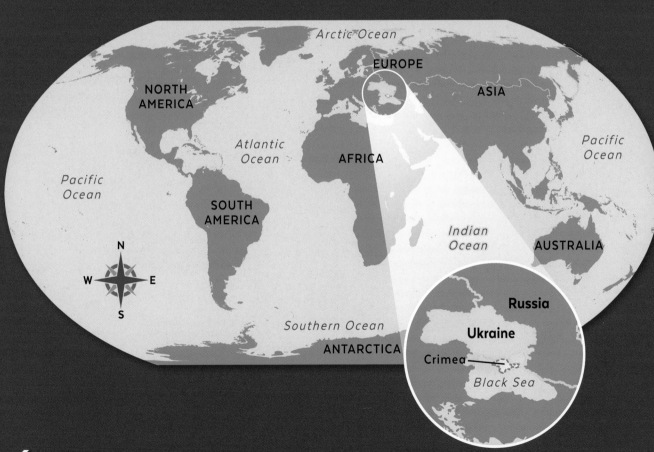

Yalta, a city in Crimea

In 2014, Russia **invaded** Crimea. This land is in southern Ukraine. Russia and Ukraine continue to fight for control of Crimea.

Most of Ukraine is flat.
Tall grasses cover much of the land.

This flat, grassy area is called a steppe.

There are mountains in western and southern Ukraine.

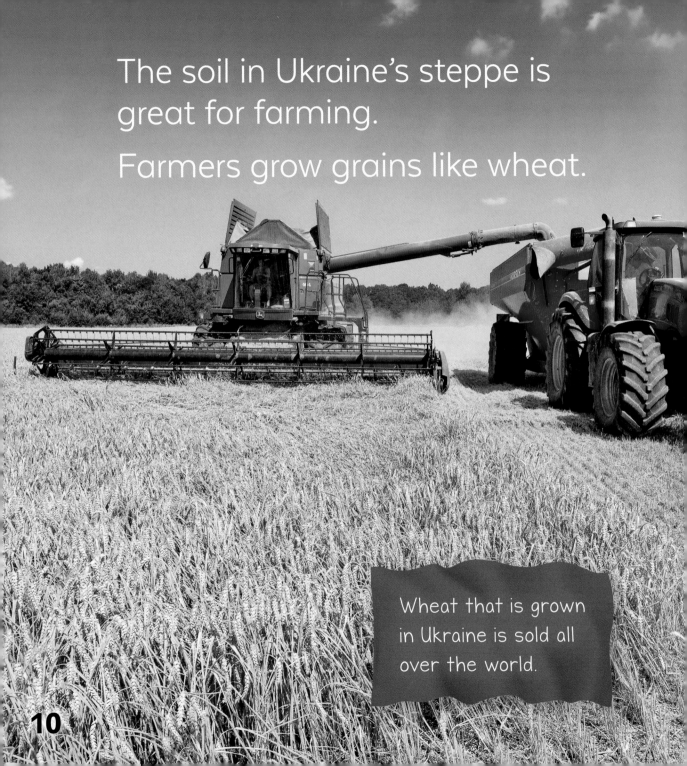

The soil in Ukraine's steppe is great for farming.

Farmers grow grains like wheat.

Wheat that is grown in Ukraine is sold all over the world.

Wheat is used to make bread.

Ukraine was once part of a huge country called the Soviet Union.

Life was difficult for Ukrainians under Soviet rule.

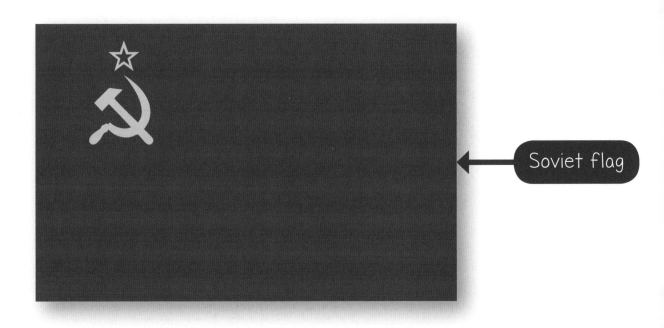

Soviet flag

In 1991, the Soviet Union broke apart.

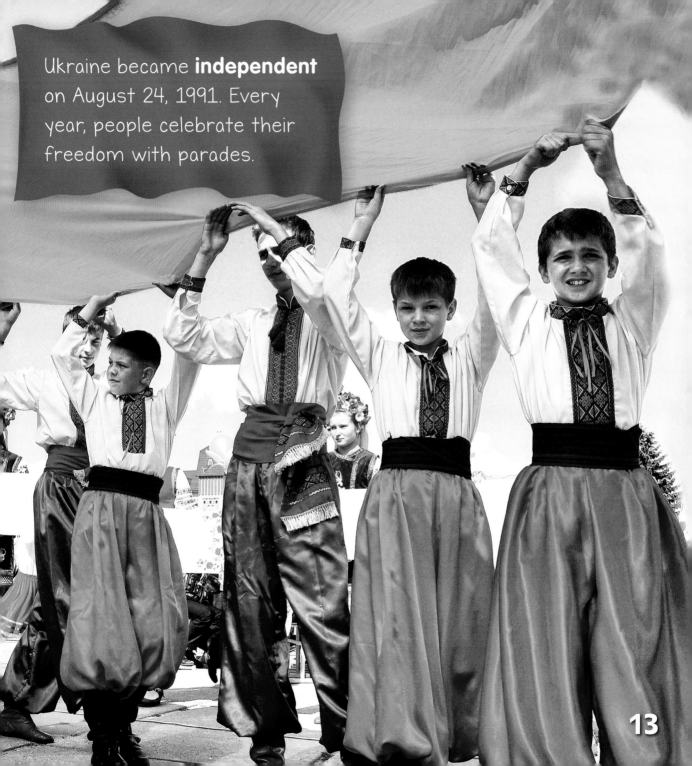

Ukraine became **independent** on August 24, 1991. Every year, people celebrate their freedom with parades.

In 1986, the world's worst **nuclear** accident occurred in Pripyat, Ukraine.

The Chernobyl power plant exploded.

Many people became sick from **radiation**.

Everyone in the town had to move away.

There are still no people living in Pripyat. However, animals such as wolves and moose have moved into the area.

Kiev is the **capital** of Ukraine.

It's also the biggest city.

Kiev can also
be spelled Kyiv.

Almost three million people live there.

Odessa is another large city in Ukraine.

Many **tourists** come to Odessa for its sunny beaches.

They love to swim in the Black Sea.

Animals like dolphins and jellyfish live in the Black Sea.

Ukrainian is the official language of Ukraine.

This is how you say *hi* in Ukrainian:

Pryvit (pree-VYET)

This is how you say *yes*:

Tak (TAHK)

Many people in Ukraine also speak Russian.

21

Ukrainians celebrate many holidays.

On Christmas, people go from house to house singing songs.

For Easter, people decorate eggs and give them as gifts.

Ukrainian people enjoy traditional dances.

Hopak is the national dance of Ukraine.

Female hopak dancers circle and swing around. The male dancers leap and kick quickly.

25

What else do Ukrainians love? Soccer!

The most popular soccer team is called Dynamo Kyiv.

Many famous athletes are from Ukraine. Vitali Klitschko is known for never having been knocked down in a boxing match.

Ukrainians make lots of yummy foods.

Vereniki are dumplings.

They can be filled with cheese, fish, or fruit.

People also eat borscht.

This is a red soup made from beets.

Chicken Kiev is chicken stuffed with butter. The meal is named after Ukraine's capital.

Fast Facts

Capital city: Kiev

Population of Ukraine:
More than 45 million

Main language:
Ukrainian

Money: Hryvnia

Major religion:
Christianity

Neighboring countries include:
Russia, Belarus, Poland, and Moldova

Cool Fact: Ukraine won several medals at the 2016 Summer Olympics. In men's gymnastics, Oleg Verniaiev won the gold medal in the parallel bars.

Glossary

capital (KAP-uh-tuhl) a city where a country's government is based

independent (in-duh-PEN-duhnt) free from control by others

invaded (in-VAYD-id) entered by force or took over

nuclear (NOO-klee-ur) having to do with a type of energy that is produced by splitting atoms

radiation (*ray*-dee-AY-shuhn) a kind of powerful energy that can be very dangerous when not properly controlled

tourists (TOOR-ists) people who travel and visit places for fun

31

Index

animals 15, 19
Black Sea 6, 18–19
cities 14–15, 16–17,
   18–19, 29, 30
dance 24–25

farming 10–11
food 11, 28–29
history 7, 12–13,
   14–15
holidays 13, 22–23

land 7, 8–9, 10, 18
language 20–21, 30
population 6, 30
sports 26–27, 30

Read More

Borgert-Spaniol, Megan. *Ukraine (Exploring Countries).* Minneapolis, MN: Bellwether Media (2014).

Kent, Deborah. *Ukraine (Enchantment of the World).* New York: Children's Press (2015).

Learn More Online

To learn more about Ukraine, visit
www.bearportpublishing.com/CountriesWeComeFrom

About the Author

Anastasiya Vasilyeva lives in New York City.
She plans to visit the beautiful city of Kiev one day.